Country Flying

HOW TO FLY FROM A PRIVATE FIELD
AND OPERATE A GROUP AIRCRAFT

by

GEOFF FARR

ROBERT POOLEY
ENGLAND

ROBERT POOLEY LIMITED
ELSTREE AERODROME, HERTFORDSHIRE,
LONDON.

Printed by Livesey Ltd., Shrewsbury.

Photographs by David Lindop
Cartoons by Jim Parry
Diagrams by Martin Bourne

For Vernon Williamson

without whose field I
could not fly.

Contents

The Author and G-ASPF

Introduction

Every private pilot's dream is to operate his own aircraft from a farm strip. This book is my account of doing just this.

After five years of operating Jodel D120 G—ASPF from a farm strip in the heart of the Cheshire countryside, I feel that the lessons learned should be passed on for the benefit of those contemplating, striving for, or maybe even dreaming of enjoying such delights.

It may be that others have solved the problems in different ways and I hope that readers will improve upon the ideas contained herein.

I offer this work as being my solution to the problems.

* * *

There is one important aspect of country flying which I have purposely avoided and this is Planning Permission.

I took advice on this matter and came to the conclusion that it is so complex and variable from district to district that I might cause more propblems than I solve.

I have successfully argued that flying from a field does not require permission for change of use if the main use of the field remains agricultural.

This does mean that you may not fence off the strip or mow it in isolation from the rest of the field.

Erecting a hangar however is an entirely different matter.

Many people who fly from farm strips do so without planning permission but without drawing upon themselves the attention of the planning authorities. I therefore decided to leave well alone.

The Aviator and his Farmer

1 The Aviator and his Farmer

To parody a well known cookery book, 'First catch your farmer'.

Unless you are lucky enough to *be* a farmer with land suitable for a light aeroplane you must first find a suitable field and then set out to discover whether its owner would be kindly disposed towards your plan.

Finding the field must be done from the air, so you hire one of the flying club's aircraft and you look. While you are looking you *do not* examine every prospect from 250 feet or practice landing upon it. That is illegal and likely to get the owner's fur up before you've even talked to him.

"Aah!!" I hear you say "There are no suitable fields near my home". Well, there were no suitable fields near mine either, until I went to find them. During the barnstorming era between the wars a suitable field was found near every small town and their machines were little different from ours.

Furthermore, though I am based upon one field I have at least four satellite fields all within a few miles upon which I have landed (with the owner's permission of course) in order to satisfy myself that they are suitable and may be used in emergency.

What emergencies could arise? Well I did once arrive back over the home field to find the muck spreaders going vigorously about their business!

Your farmer, when you find him should be a dairy or mixed farmer. You want a grass field, so an arable farmer is no good to you. He might want to change his crop next year to barley or some other crop equally incompatible with your aeroplane. He should also, for preference, be farming a large acreage (not less than 250 acres) and be running a good sized dairy herd.

What has that to do with flying from his field? Well, it comes back to needing a grass field and your best bet in obtaining the use of one is finding a field that is used not as you may think for pasture, but for winter feed.

Having obtained your farmer's consent to the use of one of his fields and established your presence upon it there are a few simple rules for maintaining your friendship with him.

You should do nothing to annoy his neighbours, because if they begin to complain you are skating on very thin ice. Flying too low over their herds or waking them from their Sunday afternoon nap will soon get you talked about, and you don't want that.

Don't be tempted to drive your car across his fields unless the ground is really hard. A car will do far more damage to a field than an aeroplane.

Don't leave gates open, unless you find them open. If you park your car in his farmyard, leave the key in it so that it can be moved if required.

If you are flying away on a trip lasting a few days, make a point of telling him or he may be concerned when you do not reappear before dark.

Discourage airborne or car-borne visitors unless you are there to receive them. It is not fair to expect your farmer to be responsible for helping clumsy aviators down from oak trees. He has his work to do.

It should be pointed out to prospective airborne visitors that no responsibility is accepted for their safety and they land entirely at their own risk.

Another obvious factor in maintaining your friendship is to choose a very quiet aeroplane or modify the one you have until it *is* quiet, for he is not likely to be enthusiastic about being on the receiving end of a Banshee howl every time you turn the wick up.

One last thing. When a farmer pays a social visit to his neighbour, he is likely to be invited to come and look at his litter of pigs, or perhaps he might be asked to view and give his opinion of this field of cabbages or the new tractor. But if his host can astonish and please his visitor with the sight of something as amazing as an aeroplane, then his stock can rise to new heights. Therefore, if your farmer brings his guests to the hangar, you will do yourself and your farmer a good turn by stopping whatever you are doing and make them welcome.

According to their degree of interest you should give them the complete tour of the aircraft with a few personal anecdotes thrown in for good measure. Your farmer will be pleased with you for entertaining his guests and your public relations job will not be wasted.

Speaking of waste, which all farmers hate, I once had a conversation with a farmer friend at a full dress function. My friend complained that the passage of time was eroding the fit of his dinner suit, especially around his spreading waist line. The suit, as is the way of dinner suits was not wearing out, though it was clear that its days were numbered. He explained that a lounge suit could be brought into everyday use for milking when its "Best Suit" days were over without arousing too much unwelcome attention, but you do feel stupid when the vet catches you ploughing in a dinner suit!

2 The Aviator and his Grass

Grass has always seemed to me to be the most forgiving medium for the aviator. Nevertheless, before flying for the first time into your farmer's field you should check the performance of yourself and your aircraft on the grass.

In order to ensure that you practice takes place in conditions you will regularly encounter, the practice should take place in nil wind conditions with a passenger and full tanks.

I did my practice on the grass beside the hard runway of my flying club, by laying down two brightly coloured anoraks representing the length of the farmer's field. It was not until I was certain of my capabilities that I attempted a landing in the field I presently occupy.

It is strange after several years to remember that I needed four or five attempts to land before finally screeching to a halt twenty five yards from the upwind fence. The nearness of fences and trees can be very off-putting to the unitiated. I now fly in and out at will and rarely need to overshoot, though I am not too proud to do so if the need arises.

So, if you find the first landings a bit hairy, don't despair, the necessary skill will soon come. The fore-going also applies to the question of cross-wind landings, which will soon become reduced from a fearful prospect to a minor inconvenience. You may one day be faced, as I was, with making a landing upon the single narrow runway at Stauning in Jutland with a 35 knot, 90° cross wind. It was not a good landing. My flying instructor would have called it an arrival, but my wife and I alighted from a still complete aeroplane, which could not be said for everybody that day.

This business of carrying out inaugural flights into grass fields can be interesting. In addition to my own inagural flights I have been asked on occasion to do them for friends who are wishing to establish a flying strip. After four attempts to land at one strip, in a strong 90° cross wind, my passenger, an experienced pilot, suggested quite forcibly that we return home and try again another day. I persisted against this strong advice and eventually made a very bad landing, only to discover that we had been trying to land downhill, a fact which would have been obvious if I had taken the precaution of walking the ground.

I have previously written that you should look for a field which is used to grow winter feed for the cows. The universal winter feed for cows in this modern farming era is silage. This is fine chopped, compressed green grass which is cut when young and tender. Often three cuts are taken during a summer. Therefore it is not left to grow long and coarse. Cutting and carrying this grass is usually accomplished in a 24 to 36 hour period, so it does not lie about too long getting tangled with your wheels. The grass usually begins to grow vigorously towards the middle of April and becomes a nuisance to the aviator about the middle of May. You can expect a two week lay-off from flying at about this time until the first cut is taken. You are in the long grass again by the end of June and can expect your second lay-off at this time. If the first two cuts give good crops and the silage barns are full, the cows will be turned out to eat the rest of the summer's crop. This does not mean that the cows will be in the field all the time since a herd of cows will eat a good crop of grass from a field in two or three days. The cows will in fact be moved in rotation around a group of fields until October when they will be taken up and housed for the winter. In either case the field is likely to be the aviator's alone from October until April because the grass won't be growing anyway. You see growth ceases when the temperature falls below 45°F. By the way it is usual to plough and re-seed a grass field every eight years because the types of grass seed currently in common use crop vigorously for eight seasons and then their peak performance is passed. You might enquire before building you hangar, when the next re-seeding is due, for you won't be flying from a ploughed field.

People at flying clubs seem to get panicky if the grass is not kept like a bowling green, however I see no reason why the determined aviator need be put off by longish grass if he is prepared to be a little adventurous in developing a few different techniques. Wet grass gives considerably more drag than dry. Before attempting to take off it can be well worth while to make two or three fast runs up and down the field in order to blow water from the grass. But beware of filling the pitot head with water or grass seeds. The ability to fly by attitude without an airspeed indicator has given me cause for satisfaction on a couple of occasions.

I have found that excessive wheel drag from long grass, mud, surface water, or snow can keep you firmly on the ground even if you have 10 miles of runway and that changes in the load of the aircraft and can make enormous difference to take off performance. I have, whilst carrying a passenger, been obliged to abandon a take off run at 400 yards when acceleration had ceased and taken off easily in 200 yards when the passenger alighted.

A ski ramp is used by the Navy to launch its' Harriers from ships. You can borrow this technique by using a hump in your field at the take off point. It does work and you can defeat the pull of quite long grass. Extensive use of satellite fields may be made in the long grass season. If arrangements are made to pick up fuel and passengers at a satellite field there are very few occasions when you will be completely stuck in the long grass and you should remember that your go or no-go decison can be left a little later, since the long grass will stop you *very* quickly if you choose to abandon your take off.

I would add, that I have not used any of the foregoing tricks with a high wing aeroplane and suspect that the high disposition of the wing weight could cause problems. It is of course essential that you should carefully conduct your own experiments with your own aeroplane and by so doing *gradually* increase your own experience. Experience of this sort should be gained gradually and not all in one morning.

A word about grass which is cut and lying would not come amiss at this point. I regard grass in this situation to be far more dangerous than grass which is long and standing. The grass, when it is cut is left lying in swathes or rows to 'wilt', that is, to lose a proportion of its natural water content. This process usually takes about 24 hours. The farmer will usually cut in one afternoon as much as he is able to pick up the following afternoon. Should I arrive back over the home field when it is part cut, I will elect every time to land in the uncut section. The reason for this is that the loose grass will build up under the wheels and can bring you to a very sudden stop. If you attempt to take off through lying grass you may place your wheels either side of a swathe, but your tail or nose wheel will be right in it. I have known it to

▲ *Approaching 35*

17

Coming in: low over the Boundary Fence

build up under the tail wheel until the rear fuselage is sitting upon a mini hay stack and, despite full power, the aeroplane was going nowhere.

The strip does not have to be perfectly level and smooth. If you have visited the Long Mountain strip at Welshpool you will know that their 800 yard (732 metres) strip is both sloping and undulating. The slope amounts to 100 feet giving a gradient of one in twenty four. Many prospective visiting aeroplanes come for a look and rapidly depart without attempting to land, yet for many years a Tiger Moth (no brakes) has been operated from the Long Mountain in complete safety. Except in the strongest winds they simply land uphill and take off downhill.

In hilly country and in close proximity to a clump of trees close attention should be given to the exploration of wind gradients, deflections and downdraughts.

How long a grass strip do you need?

We have two strips 27/09 is 560 yards (513 metres) 35/17 is 530 yards (485 metres). The hangar is located beside 27/09. When 35/17 in a neighbouring field is used, a piece of specially made tubular steel fence is withdrawn from sleeves set in the ground. An aeroplane cannot of course be taken through a conventional farm gate.

Both strips have been found to be adequate for all occasions except in the case of extremely long grass.

Visitors have included Piper Colt, Jodels of various marks, Taylor Monoplane, Fred, Emeraude, Tipsy Nipper and Minicab.

Most pilots have had little difficulty, though those accustomed to one thousand yards of concrete runway have had to re-adjust themselves to coming over the boundary fence at about 10 feet.

Approaching 17

Approaching 27 ▼

20

People have told me of operating aircraft from 350 yards of grass, but I would consider that unwise for regular movements in a variety of conditions.

We are usually airborne at the halfway mark or very soon after, and the landing run usually ends about 150 — 200 yards from the upwind fence.

It is also a good idea to make a habit of walking your strips fairly regularly, especially if the muck spreaders have been out. The handling and spreading of muck is done entirely mechanically and it is not unusual to find that the spreader has laid in your path half a fence post or maybe a house brick. This is of course fairly well disguised by a liberal coating of the spreader's main cargo!

The Aviator and his Grass

Refuelling

3 The Aviator and his Fuel

It is usual when operating from a private strip to fly to the nearest flying club or municipal airfield for regular supplies of fuel, but he would be an imprudent aviator who did not have a suitably, safely and legally stored reserve of fuel at his home base.

Transferring your fuel from your 5 gallon metal (not PVC as these can generate a dangerous charge of static electricity), cans will easily be accomplished by carrying your refuelling yoke to your aeroplane, placing both your cans upon the platform. The delivery hose is placed in the tank, the suction hose placed in the can and about 25 strokes of your pump will transfer four gallons of fuel.

The pump I use is a "Whale" pump, model Gusher 10 Mark III reference BP 37 and is manufactured by:—

Munster Simms Engineering Ltd.,
Old Belfast Road,
Bangor,
Co. Down,
N. Ireland.

These pumps are often used as bilge pumps for canal cruisers and so are obtained at marine stores.

The pump has an anodised diecast alloy body coated with epoxy resin. The handle is stainless steel and the diaphragm can be supplied in neoprene or nitrile. This latter should be specified as it absorbs less petrol and will therefore have a longer life. The weight of the pump is only five pounds and the manufacturers say it will move up to 18 gallons per minute and uses suction and delivery hoses of 1½″ bore.

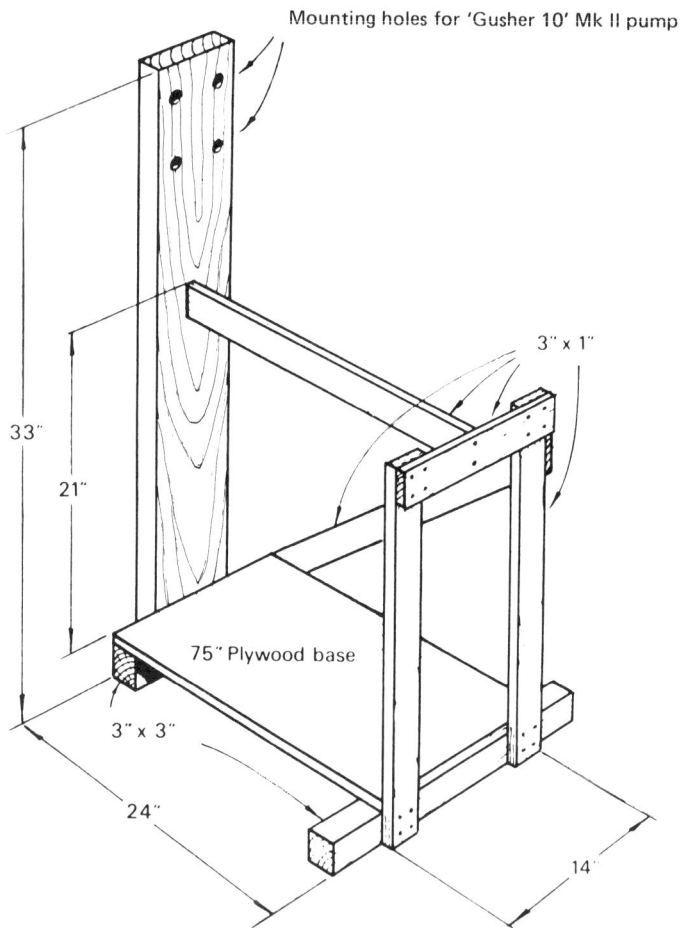

Mounting holes for 'Gusher 10' Mk II pump

3" x 1"

33"

21"

75" Plywood base

3" x 3"

24"

14"

Refuelling Yoke

24

If you are right handed the re-fuelling yoke shown will serve you well. Should you be left handed reverse the diagonal brace and foot rest.

The filtration plant consists of several layers of nylon tights securely wired with stainless locking wire over the open ends of suction and delivery hoses.

I find that if you leave about half a gallon of fuel in your five gallon can, you also leave dirt, water or sediment with it.

If like me, you have renewed windscreen or side-screens with Lexan or Makralon, don't splash them with petrol or they will melt.

Engine oil is best purchased in 25 litre drums which are bored and tapped at the base for the provision of a tap. The oil may then be drawn off as required.

"Have you been at the hard stuff again?"

The aviator and his cow

4 The Aviator and the Cow

The first thing to realise about the cow is that it was her field before it was yours. Therefore it is she who is tolerating you. All her little foibles, like calving on your runway must be seen in this light, so she must be given precedence in all circumstances at all times.

She does enjoy a good scratch. A fence post is good for rubbing her neck and so is your aeroplane. If your aeroplane is made of wood and fabric she is just as likely to eat it. The best you can hope for of an un-supervised encounter, is to have your aeroplane thoroughly licked and, with a tongue like hers, she can lick the enamel off a car – as many an angler has discovered after a carefree day fishing. So don't go home for your lunch leaving an unguarded aeroplane until you have asked your farmer which field he will turn her into after milking.

By and large milking cows do not constitute a great hazard, they can be curious of course, but their main concern is cropping the grass and they don't take a great deal of notice of taxiing aeroplanes. But there is always one in a herd who can become belligerent. So, unless your taxiing route can be kept well clear, you *do* need someone walking in front to clear the way.

Should you ever arrive over the home field to find it full of cows you can, with a few well directed low passes, herd them onto one side before making your landing, but do beware of the odd one left by herself. She is certain to feel lonely and choose the very moment of your landing to cross the strip and join her sisters. I would advise an out-of-wind landing on a neighbouring field, if this is possible.

The most troublesome cows are the young ones, yearlings, heifers or followers, they may be called. These are the females being reared to take their place in the milking herd. These, like their human counterparts, have an insatiable curiosity and are eager to participate in the most bizarre schemes, like trying to pull down your windsock, or trying by the dozen to crop the grass behind the hangar where there is room for only two.

They are often left out during the winter except for the most severe weather. The combination of a good November rain and their feet can cut up a field more completely and more devastatingly than anything I know.

Having discoursed at some length about what goes into the cow, we must inevitably come to the question of what comes out. Yes!! I know about about milk, but that is not usually left in the path of the unsuspecting aviator.

Cow muck is a most unpleasant substance, but not to everyone. I am reminded of a veterinary friend who was commiserating with me upon the recent cold weather in which I am obliged to earn my living. I said that his job might be considered by some to be unpleasant. "Nonsense ' was his reply, "At least when I have my arm up a cows' rear end it *is* warm."

Be that as it may, I still do not like cow muck plastered upon the underside of my aeroplane, hot or cold. Removing the wretched stuff from a rag aeroplane is a bore and a trial.

If the aeroplane is a Jodel, it may be gently lifted stern to wind (light breeze only) until the air intake rests upon something soft which you have placed upon

Washing the underside

the ground. You must tie a piece of rope to the tail wheel in order to steady the operation as the weight moves forward of the main wheels and also to pull the tail down to earth when washing is completed.

Using a household scrubbing brush, hot water and washing up liquid you will eventually remove the troublesome mess, but not before you have run liberal quantities of water up your sleeves and into your wellingtons.

A comical by-product of the process will be the number of people who rush up to see why you crashed, since a Jodel standing upon its nose looks like a nasty accident which has recently happened.

5 Handling and Protecting your Flying Machine

The only good defence I know for a hangar or an aeroplane is the electric fence. It has the twin attributes of being very mobile and very cheap.

You simply push the insulated rods into the ground at about twenty or twenty five foot intervals. Hang the wire through the eye at the top of each rod and connect the battery operated fencer to the wire. You will hear the fencer pulsing and check the warning lights to satisfy yourself as to the condition of the battery and that the wire is not accidentally earthed.

How can you be sure it is working before you depart? Well!! you should take a blade of grass and hold one end of the grass upon the electrified wire. At each pulse you will feel the faintest tingle which will cause you no discomfort but will convince you that the fence is working.

A fencer dry battery will cost in the teens of pounds, but will last for a year or longer.

You have to arrange things so that you are able to move your aeroplane in and out of your hangar unaided. You may be alone or with an uninitiated passenger who is sure to push when you wish him to pull and hangar rash could well result. The resistance to the rolling of the wheels upon the grass or soft earth is very much greater than upon a hard surface. This is never more noticable than when you are trying single handed to roll the aeroplane out of the hangar to a place sufficiently distant to safely start the engine. Whether your aero plane is a tricycle with a pull handle or a tail dragger, it can be an almost impossible task to accomplish without straining to the point where your shirt buttons fly off, or as happened to me your feet shoot from under you leaving you sitting rather uncomfortably in a freshly laid cow pat. Climbing back to your feet smelling evilly the simple solution dawns on you. You must arrange your hangar floor to slope upwards from front to back This, together with three lines of paving slabs, 24 inches wide laid with their tops level with the surface of the ground so that the mowing machine won't strike them. If each line of slabs is, say ten yards out from the hangar entrance, you can pull the machine out to the extent of the pavings and then turn it through ninety degrees to start up. To hangar the aeroplane, I have anchored a small boat winch in the back of the hangar. Using a claw on the end of the cable, the aeroplane is easily winched uphill into the hangar

G-ASPF 'Snug and dry'

6 The Aviator and his Hangar

When you contemplate your hangar design the main points to consider are as follows. These are not listed in order of priority since everyone's priorities are different.

1. Cost.
2. Structural Integrity.
3. Portability.
4. Ease of construction.
5. Convenience for working in.
6. Ease of maintenance of the building.

Cost consideration needs no explanation from me. Neither does structural integrity except to say that professionally built hangars often suffer in high winds as I am sure you will remember from the nationwide damage to hangars and aeroplanes during the strong winds on the night of 1st and 2nd January, 1976.

The weakest part of most small hangars is the doors and their hangings.

My hangar design has no doors and this obviates the necessity to construct troublesome hangings, though we do of course have total enclosure.

As to portability. Your tenancy of the field is likely to be of grace and favour nature, rather than a legal tenancy. Therefore if your farmer should have to ask you to leave, you must be able to quickly remove your hangar to another location.

Ease of Construction
Well, I am basically lazy and any effort which can be avoided must be avoided. I'm sure you agree.

Convenience for Working In

You will be lucky if you are able to have electricity or heating. If you plan without it you won't be disappointed. I have spent many hours during 'brass-monkey' weather working not very fruitfully, since when your hands are frozen it takes a long time to complete the simplest task, as you who have skinned your fingers with a slipping spanner on a frosty morning will agree.

The light problem is simply overcome since my hangar sheeting is translucent, giving me complete daylight in any part of the hangar.

Bird droppings upon the aeroplane seem to be a problem in conventionally roofed hangars. The abundance of light seems to make them feel insecure so they do not take up residence, either for resting or Winter roost.

For peering into the dark depths of the fuselage, I use an old motorcycle headlamp powered by a car battery.

Ease of Maintenance

This comes back to being lazy and anyway who wants to waste good flying weather painting the hangar.

So, choose your materials and building techniques with care.

Siting the hangar can be very important. It must of course be placed where it will not be a continuous nuisance to the farmer. Mowing around it could be time consuming.

Economy of space is also important. This means that a corner is usually best, but it must not be the lowest corner, or it may be the wettest after a downpour. So, ask a few questions about the subsoil drainage in the vicinity of the proposed site and do not spoil any sub-soil drains with your foundation works, or you may live to regret it.

If you place your hangar so that farm buildings lie between it and the farmhouse, you will spare the farmer the noise of your engine run up.

Some shrubbery between the highway and the hangar might save you a visit from vandals.

As regards shelter from the winds, I have found that an uninterrupted gale crossing an open field is less destructive than one which is deflected between and around neighbouring buildings.

If some of these siting hints seem to contradict each other, do not be too concerned since beggars can't be choosers, so you will be lucky if you are offered a spot which covers half of these criteria.

Constructing your Hangar

Mark a base line on the workshop floor to represent the ground level. Now, mark full size the front profile of the aeroplane to be housed as if it were sitting upon the ground.

Let us say that the aeroplane stands 6 feet 6 inches high at the highest point. To give allowances for settlement and probably the opening upwards of the canopy (Jodel style) mark the apex at least 8 feet above ground level. Describe a suitable curve (outwards and downwards from the centre high point) which will clear the wing tips by 6 – 8 inches. The portion from wing-tip to ground may be allowed to descend steeply.

You now have the outline of your trusses, which you will make in two halves, sleeved at the centre for bolting-up on site.

The trusses themselves are constructed from 2 inch overall diameter mild steel tubes cut into short lengths (see drawings) and welded together upon the floor markings to obtain uniformity.

Allow at the ground end an extra 6 inches because when you erect the trusses, you will set padstones into the ground to spread the weight. These padstones will be set at an angle to oppose the thrust which will want to spread the legs. You must give some thought at this stage to the possibility of laying a wooden floor to keep the aeroplane off the ground. I used some old garage doors for this purpose, they work very well, but a height allowance must be made.

You should reckon on needing a truss about every four feet, six inches. So, for a Jodel which is about twenty-two feet long, you will need six trusses. Do not be tempted to make a tee hangar reducing in width behind the wings. The amount of work involved is enormous. The savings in materials minimal and the consequent space is cramped.

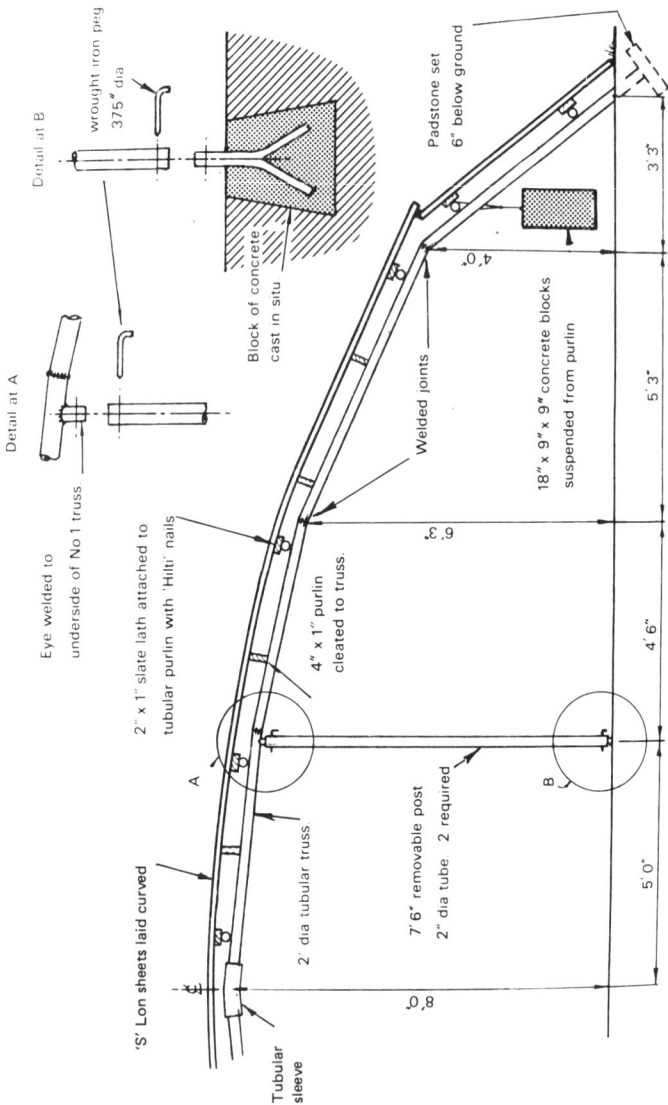

Detail at B

wrought iron peg
.375" dia

Block of concrete
cast in situ

Detail at A

Eye welded to
underside of No 1 truss

2" x 1" slate lath attached to
tubular purlin with 'Hilti' nails

Padstone set
6" below ground

Welded joints

18" x 9" x 9" concrete blocks
suspended from purlin

4" x 1" purlin
cleated to truss

'S' Lon sheets laid curved

2" dia tubular truss.

7'6" removable post
2" dia tube 2 required

Tubular
sleeve

A

B

3' 3"

4' 0"

5' 3"

6' 3"

4' 6"

5' 0"

8' 0"

Cross-sectional view showing constructional details of hangar

38

My hangar was built this way and I have cursed my short-sighted stupidity ever since. It may also be worth mentioning that my first effort at building a hangar was a dismal failure. If you should be tempted to stretch tarpaulin or PVC sheets over a framework of scaffolding tubes, forget it. This method totally ignores the power of the wind which will certainly take your sheeting away and may even take your aeroplane with it. BE WARNED.

When you have made your trusses, take them to the site and bolt the halves together. Set your padstones in the ground. Pieces of paving slab will do admirably, provided they are large enough to spread the weight without sinking.

Set up the trusses and prop them.

Take a length of tube as long as the hangar and lock it along the top of the trusses, from front to back of the hangar. Scaffold clips should be used for these attachments. Place a tube as above on each side of the hangar at the joint which approximates to the wing tip. You should now have a structure which is capable of standing unaided.

The three horizontal tubes that you have just used to lock the structure are called 'Purlins', and must be thin walled tube of the same diameter as that used for the trusses or you will not be able to use scaffold-clips for the joints, and this of course is the answer to the need for portability.

I have used some very rusty, very old scrap scaffolding tubes which serve admirably.

Why thin walled tubes? Well, you have to attach two-inch by one-inch slate lathes to the purlins and you may do this easily with 'Hilti' nails.

Hilti steel nails are designed to be fixed using .22 blank cartridges and a special gun, into steel or concrete.

If, however, you use thin walled tubing and a heavy hammer, you will not need either cartridges or gun.

The roofing sheets should be 'S Lon' 24 mm corrugated translucent, self extinguishing, rigid PVC sheets. These are available in six, eight and ten foot lengths.

The purlins need to be set about 2 feet apart with slate lathes nailed to the top of each. The sheets will be heavily nailed at about 6 inches centres with waterproof washers to the slate lathes, with care being taken not to squeeze the corrugations by overdriving the nails.

In order to accommodate the curve of the roof the 'S Lon' sheets will have to be bent. This is done by commencing the nailing at one end and progressing to each purlin in turn. Thus, by pre-stressing, the resultant curve in the sheet makes it stronger than the same sheet when laid flat.

Arrange the sheets so as to give at least 6 inches of lap at each joint and have no joint at the top of the curve.

An overhang of about 6 inches should be enough to form an eave at the wing tip joint. The outer sheets below the eave may be fixed without a curve because being nearly vertical they won't gather any snow.

The vertical sheeting at the back of the hangar is nailed to horizontal timbers which themselves are nailed with Hilti nails to a framework of scaffolding tubes.

At the outer edge, one of the purlins should be arranged at about 36 inches above the ground, because having described how to hold the hangar up I must now describe the method of holding it down. I can assure you that a gale will move your hangar if you don't anchor it.

My hangar was hastily modified in the following manner, a very short while after seeing it slightly airborne.

Place a 2 inch plank beneath the 36 inch high purlin. Set a row of 18 x 9 x 9 inch hollow concrete blocks on end and wire them with stout wire to the 36 inch high purlin mentioned above. Now remove the plank and leave the blocks hanging beneath the purlin.

The hangar mouth is dealt with as follows. At about four feet either side of the centre line across the hangar mouth, cast into the ground a dovetailed block of concrete.

This concrete block should have a wrought iron fish-tail cast into it with an eye showing above the block. An eye must be welded to the truss above the ground level eye. Now cut a piece of tube 2 inches diameter and two inches longer than the centres of the two eyes. Drill holes in the tube one inch from each end. These holes should now coincide with the eyes. A wrought-iron peg through each end of the erected post will tie down the hangar in a blow and strut it up under a weight of snow.

To close the hangar against the weather, send your drawing to a firm of wagon tarpaulin makers and ask them to make up your "door" of reinforced PVC of the type used to cover loads. You will need reinforced brass eyes around the perimeter at about 12 inch centres.

The sheet will be lashed with sash-cord along the roof truss and secured at the bottom with "dog lead" clips attached to the brass eyes and hooked to a wire stretched across the hangar mouth at ground level.

To open the door, release the dog-lead clips and reef the sheet up to the truss.

The door when closed is kept in good tension so that it gives help in a blow to the removable posts.

The hangar you now have should last for some years trouble free. My own has stood now for six years. It has kept my aeroplane snug and dry and has sustained the loss of just one sheet during a gale. Actually the heifers have done more damage during two or three incursions into the compound than six years of evil weather.

Since costs are constantly spiralling upwards, it seems pointless to go into details. Sufficient is it to say that one year's hangarage at a commercial airport would have cost more than the cost of materials for the building.

"Mon repos"

7 The Country Aviator and his Safety

Every aviator should be safety conscious, but the country aviator needs to be a little more safety conscious than the others. It is therefore good to have a little plan to avoid the more common dangers. You will of course carry a fire extinguisher in your aeroplane. It is a good idea to have a second one in the hangar. Since your hangar will be situated in a remote location, you can expect little immediate help in an emergency, so be prepared to help yourself. I have experienced an engine fire due to over priming for start up and the B.C.F. extinguisher paid for itself in a five second burst which instantly killed the flames.

Birch and Bramson have written that an engine fire can be quite minor (Flight Briefing for Pilots Vol. I). I laughed when I read it, but they were quite right. Due to the prompt application of B.C.F., no real damage was sustained and flying resumed shortly afterwards.

B.C.F., like CO_2, puts out the fire and very soon completely evaporates leaving no powder, foam or water to clean out of the engine and its equipment.

With considerable difficulty I landed one evening in a gale. My Danish friend following in his Emeraude made four attempts to land. The ferocity of the gale bounced him around like a cork during each attempt and I soon became convinced that there was going to be a crash. I grabbed my fire extinguisher and rushed to the threshold in order to be close at hand to haul him out of the wreckage. On the fifth attempt he landed safely, switched off his engine, opened the canopy and shouted to me

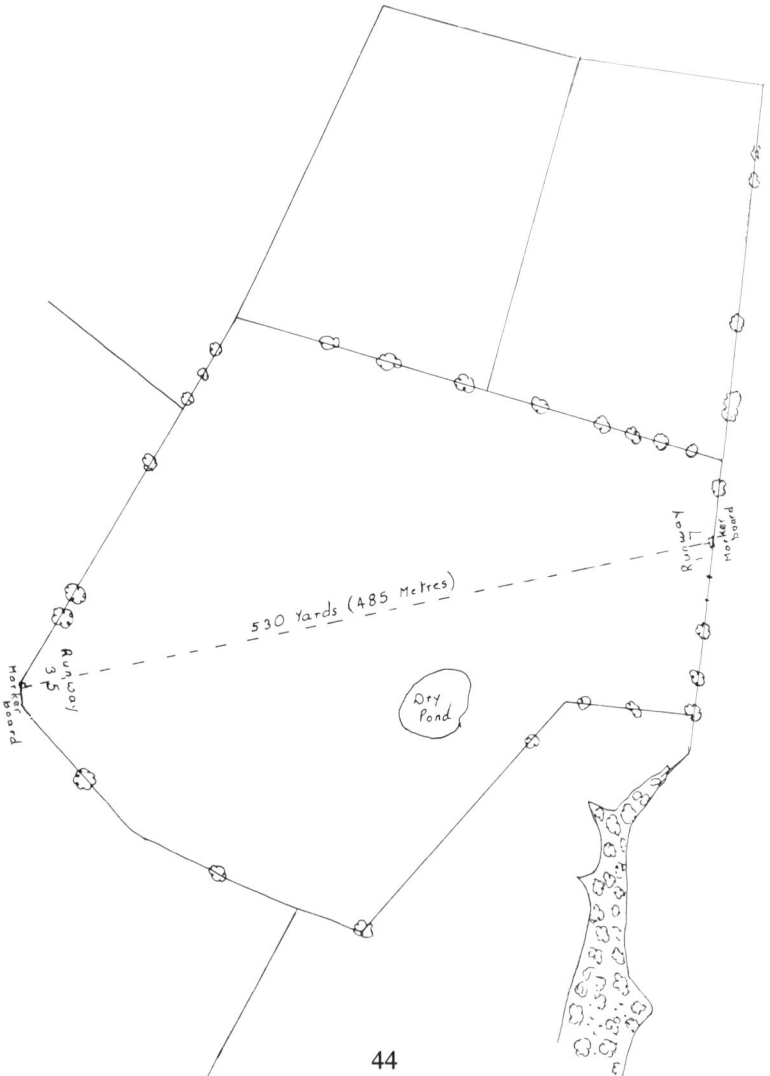

Plan of

530 Yards (485 Metres)

Dry Pond

Runway 35

Marker board

Runway Marker board

Mowing Line

Austerson Dairy Farm

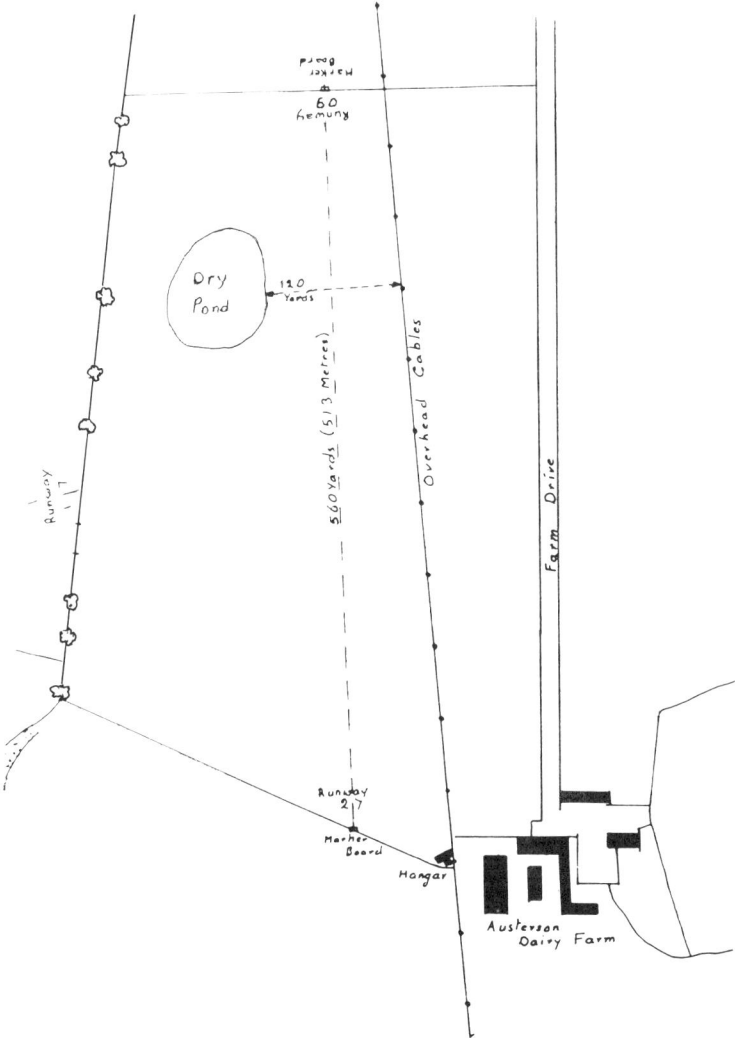

Marker board

60
Gemundy

Dry
Pond

120
Yards

Overhead Cables

Runway
17

560 Yards (513 Metres)

Farm Drive

Runway
2|7

Marker
Board

Hangar

Austerson
Dairy Farm

above the roar of the wind 'Thiss iss der flyink for men vith hair full chests".

On another occasion he arrived rather late and we had to light the runway with the lamps of three cars. His landing was rather a heavy one and his seat collapsed. Taxiing back to the hangar he tried to explain what had happened. 'You see", he said, "I have to steer from zee basement".

Power cables are an obvious hazard, but you can live with them if they are approximately parallel to your intended runway. You can, in certain circumstances, pass under them in the early part of your take off run though I would never attempt to land under them.

If they cross your path on the approach, you will soon accustom yourself to knowing when to look for them, but they *are* a hazard to visiting pilots.

Uninvited airborne visitors are at greatest risk in this respect, as you have not had an opportunity to forewarn them.

They think that they will see the hazards but often they do not. If you examine the plan of runway 27/09 you will see where the cables lie but you cannot see them on the aerial photographs of the approach to that runway.

I watched horrified on one occasion as an uninvited Auster attempted to land on a heading of 180° across the line of the power wires. The pilot saw the wires only just in time and came within an ace of stalling his Auster heaving it over them.

The incident would not have happened had he telephoned and received a briefing beforehand.

If he had crashed it is certain that neither he nor I would have flown from that field again. It may at first sight seem selfish, but I do not allow the whereabouts of my strip to be published because an abuse by some unthinking aviator may cause me to lose it.

This does not mean that I feel no good will or neighbourliness towards by fellow aviators, it simply means that it is not *my* field.

I do however leave out permanently my seven foot windsock and this is done on purpose to provide a safe haven for anyone in real distress.

On arriving at my field one Sunday morning I was somewhat surprised to see a Cherokee 140 parked beside my hangar. With darkness falling and airports all around fogged in, the pilot remembered seeing our strip and sock and sought sanctuary. In very poor visibility he landed safely and offered up a prayer. It was not an easy matter to fly the aeroplane out again some days later, but the pilot was profoundly grateful to get in.

Since the possibility of being lost is a constant companion of the aviator, it would make sense to give some thought to finding yourself before you are lost. In this connection I would suggest a placard in the aeroplane showing the Latitude and Longitude of the strip so that you can communicate it whilst in flight to anyone who may try to help you. If you carry the appropriate navigation aids if is a good idea to placard the co-ordinates of as many convenient radio navigation facilities as possible. Headings to your strip from several topographical features and landmarks are very useful luggage.

I have on several occasions been glad to have to hand:--

275º from Doddington Lake

045º from the "Combermere Arms"

A 'Record of Flights' sheet should be pinned up in the hangar so that the log may be filled in before leaving the field and details of faults may be listed for the atten-

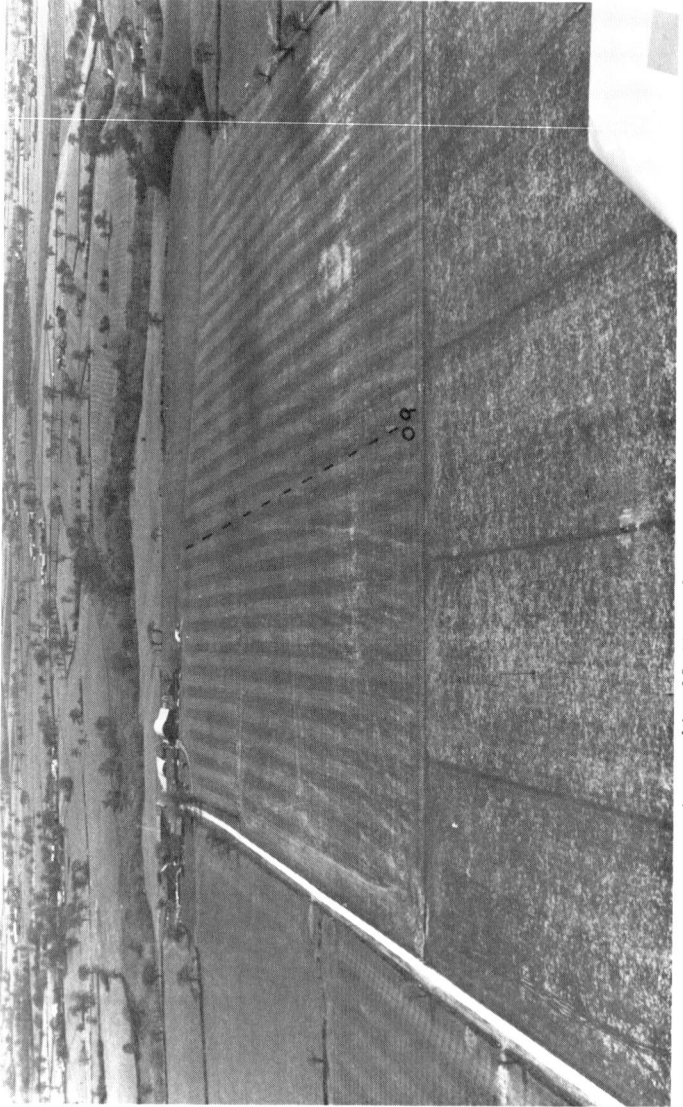

Approaching 09. Note: the power cables are not visible

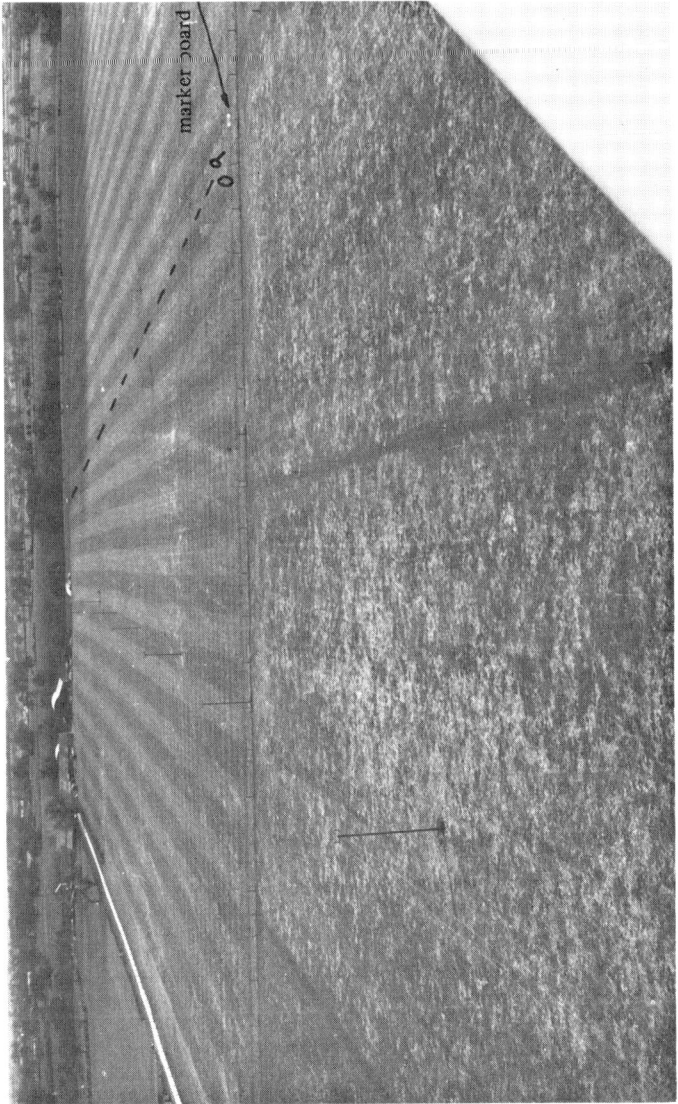

marker board

9
0

But they ARE there

tion of another pilot if the aircraft is shared. Also the sheet provides the means of booking out which should be done for safety's sake.

Extensive use should be made of the Flight Information Service. You should give them your call sign, point of departure, present position, height, flight condition (i.e. VFR or IFR), destination and E.T.A.

Since you have left a field with no services and often no one will even observe your departure, let alone know where to look if you are overdue. In these circumstances the F.I.S. may be the only people who know anything at all of your flight, and that will only be the case if you tell them. The F I.S. will also give you the area QNH and any other flight information you may need. But please, if you talk to them, don't leave them with a loose end by failing to advise them of your arrival at your destination. If, as sometimes can happen, you can't raise them upon arrival, try the other F.I.S. frequencies or even the telephone, but do let them know you are O.K.

Wheel spats are not a great deal of use to the country aviator, primarily because they do not afford enough ground clearance on a rough field and consequently they cause too much drag in even quite short grass. They also fill with mud which obstructs rotation of the wheels and adds weight. My own preference is for a pair of glass fibre mudguards of robust construction which help to keep down some of the cow muck, but remain at all times half a wheel diameter from the ground and appear to neither enhance or detract from performance.

The mudguards should be used between September and April when the field may be muddy. When the grass is growing there is usually no mud, also the mudguards

Mudguards are more practical than spats

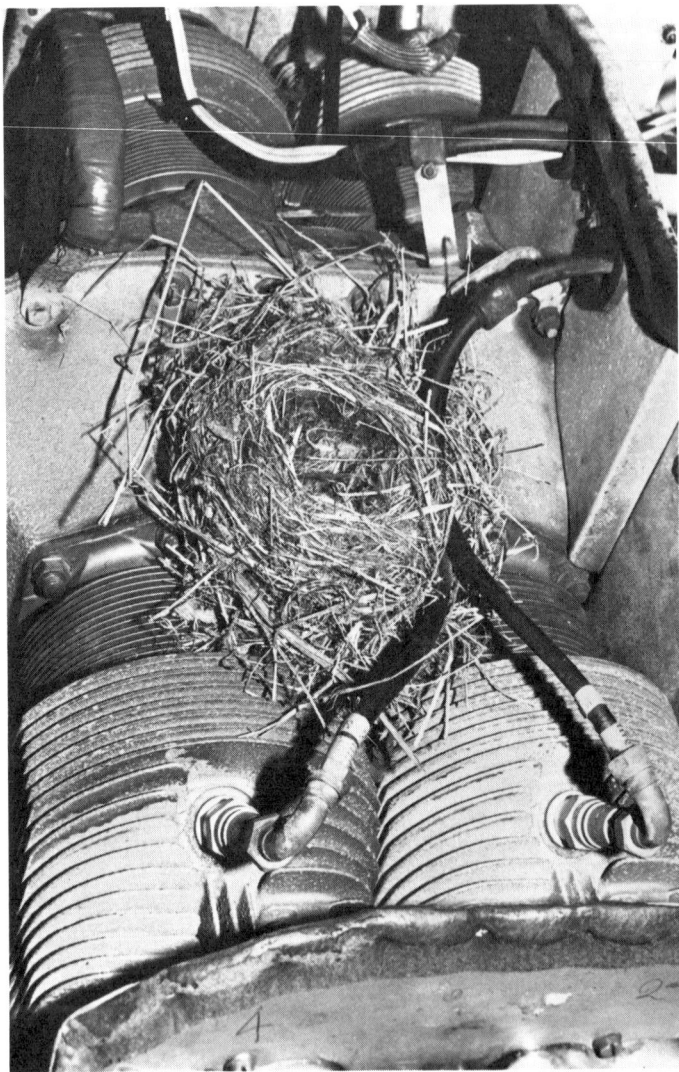

unapproved engine modification

drag in longish grass which will be your biggest summer problem.

Narrow wheels and tyres should also be avoided. Our wheels are 420 x 150 and tyres 600 x 6½. These spread the weight quite nicely and give no tendency to nose over on landing, even on the softest ground.

A few years ago the friend who shares Papa Foxtrot with me was taking off from our strip. As he climbed through four hundred feet, four Harriers in formation passed underneath him.

His reaction to this occurrence was, as you might expect, quite unprintable, and the reaction of the Harrier drivers is not on record. Though I believe five pairs of clean trousers were required shortly afterwards.

This foregoing cautionary tale illustrates another hazard to the country aviator.

The military being a law unto themselves, feel the need to fly their 'hurry-up' carts at tree top height around certain parts of the countryside. If you know a friendly military aviator chappie, he might allow you to peek under the blotting paper at his map, so that you may know whether he will be competing for your bit of sky.

You will not of course persuade him to keep out of your back yard, but armed with the knowledge you can take extra care to avoid *him*.

The chances are that he will tell you his map is private, but you never know your luck. He might possibly have driven a Harrier under a Jodel and failed to enjoy it.

8 Publications and Documents for the Country Aviator

The pre-recorded Visual Flight Forecast Service provided by the Met. Office is invaluable to country aviators. You can take your forecast over the telephone before leaving home, for you are unlikely to have a telephone in the middle of a pasture field. Also you won't need to bother the busy met. officers and, having taken a forecast, you will be legal.

If you are contemplating a long trip, perhaps even going foreign the forecast provided by the V.F.F.S. will not be sufficient, but you can ring the appropriate Class A Met. Office and ask them in advance (give them 24 hours notice) to provide a detailed forecast for you at your customs clearance airfield.

The pro forma sheets for taking down the V.F.F.S. can be obtained free from: –

Popular Flying Association,
Shoreham Airport,
Shoreham, Sussex.
Telephone: (07917) 61616.

Airtour International Ltd.,
Elstree Aerodrome,
Herts.
Telephone: 01 953 4870.

Send them a stamped addressed envelope with your request. The telephone numbers for the V.F.F.S.
Areas 10 to 16   Manchester **(061) 499 1717**
                    West Drayton **(08954) 42513**
Areas 17 to 30   Manchester **(061) 499 3131**
                    West Drayton **(08954) 49262/3**

A copy of each side of the pro-forma is reproduced showing a typical forecast: Reading it will explain everything.

Civil Aviation Authority

General Aviation Visual Flight Forecast Service

PILOT'S PROFORMA

NOTES:

1 (a) For areas 10 to 16 on the map (on reverse) telephone Manchester (061) 499-1717 or West Drayton 42513.
   (b) For areas 17 to 30 on the map (on reverse) telephone West Drayton 49262 or 49263 or Manchester (061) 439-3131.

2 As the recording is of 3 minutes duration, you are advised to ensure that you insert the appropriate coinage if using a coin operated telephone.

3 Comments on this service should be sent to C(G)3, Room T1118, CAA House, 45–59 Kingsway, London WC2B 6TE.

PERIOD OF VALIDITY	From *1400* to *2200* GMT	Date *1 / 3 / 79*

General Weather Situation *A Westerly will increase as an Atlantic warm front moves Eastwards towards Ireland. Scattered wintry showers will later turn to rain*

WARNINGS *Moderate turbulance. Moderate to severe icing in shower cloud*

FREEZING LEVEL (0°C)	Areas *10 to 16*	Height (ft) AMSL *2 to 3000 ft*

Areas	10	11	12	13	14	15	16	17	18	19	20	21	22	23	24	25	26	27	28	29	30	Categories
WEATHER																						CAVOK
	✓	✓	✓	✓	✓	✓	✓	*Tempo Mike*														O
																						D
																						M
																						x

UPPER WINDS	Areas	Direction (deg T)	Speed (kt)
2500 ft	*10 to 16*	*270*	*35*
5000 ft	*10 to 16*	*290*	*35*
7500 ft	*10 to 16*	*300*	*40*

IMPORTANT: *When in doubt about the forecast weather conditions en route, pilots are strongly advised to telephone their designated parent meteorological office for a full personal briefing by a forecaster.*

EXPLANATION OF THE WEATHER CATEGORIES USED IN THIS FORECAST

Category	Visibility	and	Cloud Base (AMSL) (4/8 or more cover)	Other Factors
CAVOK	10 km or more	and	no cloud below 5000 ft and no cumulonimbus.	No precipitation, thunderstorm, shallow fog or low drifting snow.
O (Oscar)	8 km or more	and	2000 ft or more.	
D (Delta)	3 – 8 km	and	1000 ft or more or	
	8 km or more	and	1000 ft to 2000 ft.	
M (Mike)	1·5 – 3 km	and	500 ft or more or	
	3 km or more	and	500 ft to 1000 ft.	
X (X-Ray)	Less than 1·5 km	and/or	less than 500 ft.	

DEFINITION OF ABBREVIATIONS USED

GRADU – Gradually becoming
TEMPO – Temporarily
INTER – Intermittent
RAPID – Rapid or rapidly

Note: To convert km to nm multiply by 0·54

CA 1701
250178

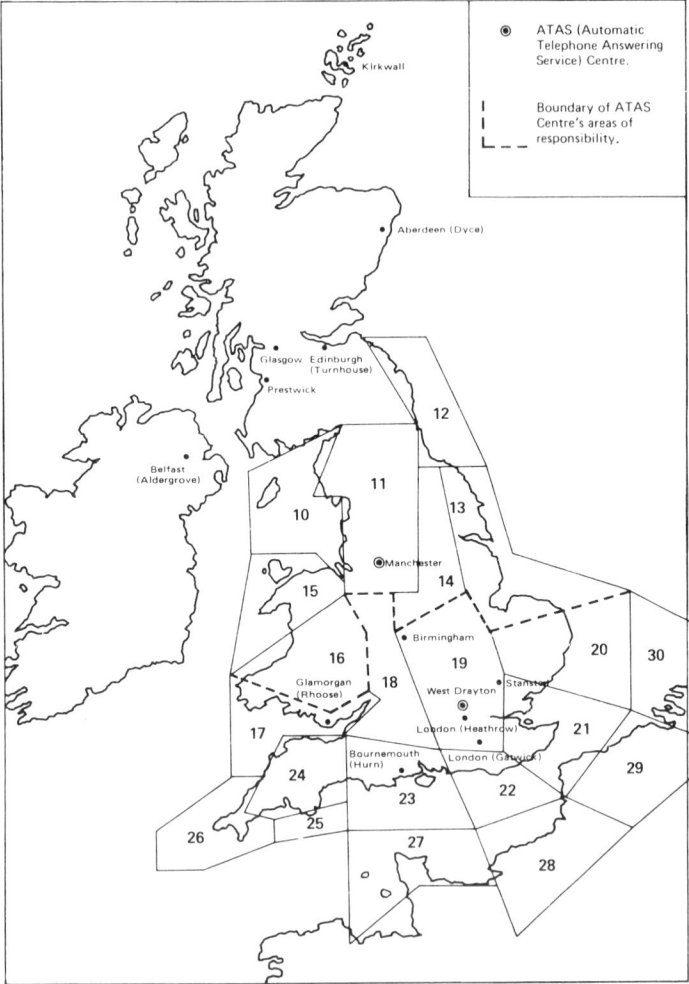

ATAS (Automatic Telephone Answering Service) Centre.

Boundary of ATAS Centre's areas of responsibility.

Kirkwall

Aberdeen (Dyce)

Glasgow Edinburgh
(Turnhouse)
Prestwick

Belfast
(Aldergrove)

12

11

10

13

Manchester

14

15

Birmingham

16

19

20

30

Glamorgan
(Rhoose)

18

West Drayton

Stansted

17

London (Heathrow)

21

24

Bournemouth
(Hurn)

London (Gatwick)

29

23

22

26

25

27

28

56

People who fly from flying clubs etc., usually have access to the club's copy of 'Air Pilot'. The Country aviator does not have access to such riches.

The best buy for the country aviator is undoubtedly Pooley's Flight Guide – United Kingdom & Ireland. This publication is produced with the assistance of the Civil Aviation Authority and is the subject of a thorough up-dating service. It should be noted however that the up-dating service applies only to the current year's copy. You must buy a new one each year. It also has the merit of being small enough to carry in your flight bag.

Many farm strips are included in Pooley's Flight Guide, but many are not and the reasons for this have been mentioned earlier in this book. No country aviator wants to see his recreation spoiled by uninvited and therefore unbriefed pilots endangering themselves, annoying farmers and causing problems with Local Councils.

The Civil Aviation Authority will (if you ask them) send to you a copy of each 'Aeronautical Information Circular' free of charge.

The Address:

C.A.A., Tolcarne Drive, Pinner, Middlesex HA5 2DU. Telephone: 01 866 8781. Ext. 259.

Information circulars are most valuable in keeping you abreast of changes in the widest variety of subjects connected with aeroplanes and their use.

United Kingdom Danger Area Charts and the Military Low Flying System Chart can also be obtained free of charge from the same address.

Airtour International, Elstree Aerodrome, Herts WD6 3AW is an alternative source of supply for U.K. Danger Area Chart and Military Low Flying System Chart on the same terms.

When you become the registered proud owner of an aeroplane, you should automatically receive a copy of each new Airworthiness Notice and loose leaf folder containing all previous notices.

Although it is not vital to be an owner, you can buy them from: —

C.A.A., Airworthiness Division, Brabazon House, Redhill, Surrey RH1 1SQ.

You will need to keep your aeroplane in A1 condition. The owner is now responsible for the condition of the machinery in the Private Category, not the engineer. Also changes in mandatory requirements appear in Airworthiness Notices. You need to know.

It was wrongly thought that 1977 would see the end of the "blood chit", the passengers waiver of claims. The flying club's exemption from the 1967 Carriage by Air Acts were withdrawn and a new act, the Unfair Contract Terms Bill was enacted. This last bill is intended to invalidate clauses in business contracts which take away rights existing in common law and that is precisely what a "blood chit" is designed to do. There are however two classes of aviators not covered by these changes. They are member's clubs and flying groups and are defined as clubs or groups in which the members jointly own and share the assets. It follows that members of groups or clubs in these circumstances cannot enter into contracts to carry passengers and therefore if passengers are carried they can only be carried as guests. Such guest passengers *can* be asked to sign a "blood chit" and by so doing they *do* legally waive the right to sue.

I reproduce a copy of our "blood chit".

G - A S P F

To: The Owner and Pilot.

I . . . . (full names in block capitals)
of (address) . . . .
Occupation . . . . Telephone No. . . . .

undertake and agree that in consideration of my being admitted as a passenger on the
above aircraft, neither I nor my heirs, executors, or administrators will make any
claim against the owner or pilot in respect of any loss of, or damage to property or
injury to person (including injury resulting in death) due to negligence or any other
cause which I may suffer while or in consequence of my being carried in the aircraft,
and I understand that no compensation will be paid by the owner in respect of such
loss or injury. Furthermore, I, so as to bind myself, my heirs, executors and
administrators, hereby indemnify the owner and pilot against any claims which may be
made by any third party against them, arising out of any act, neglect or default on
my part during or in connection with the said carriage.

Date of Birth . . . . I am   a British subject
                                   am not

Dated the . . . . day of 19

                              Signature . . . . . .

In the presence of :-

Signature of Witness . . . .
Address of Witness . . . .

DECLARATION to be signed by the Parent or Guardian of any passenger under
          the age of 21 years.

I . . . . (full name in block letters)
of (address) . . . .
Occupation . . . .

hereby declare that I am the Parent/Guardian of the Minor who has signed the
form of indemnity above. I have read and understood the terms and conditions
of this indemnity, and I agree, both on my behalf and on behalf of the above
named Minor to accept and be bound by them.

Dated the . . . . day of 19
Signed by the said . . . .

In the presence of :-

Signature of Witness . . . .
Address of Witness . . . .

Blood Chit

59

A few simple rules are necessary for the smooth operation of your group. The fewer and simpler the better. I reproduce opposite our group agreement which I have never had cause to amend or alter except of course to revise charges in the light of inflatory costs.

11.4.1973

Group Operation Agreement G-A.S.P.F.

Copies to: Mr. G. H. Farr, Mr. A. Jepson, Mr. J. Underwood and any other pilot and Insurance Company.

Contributions

The contributions for the aircraft is to be £2 per week standing charge and £4 per hour for each flying hour. These charges may be changed as agreed by the group.

Responsibilities

The pilot in charge will be responsible for the following:—

1. Flying time payments.
2. Landing charges at airfields visited.
3. Obtaining signed witnessed indemnities.
4. *All* uninsured losses.
   N.B. This includes losses from inadequate picketing.
5. Obtaining fresh supplies of fuel and oil after his flight.

Defects

Should a defect occur in any equipment the information will be telephoned to the remaining pilots without delay, and a note left in the aircraft in a prominent position.

Receipts

Receipts for fuel and oil will be accepted as part payment for flying time.

Fuel Drawback

Fuel drawback payments from foreign trips to be credited to pilot in charge.

Two copies of this document are to be sent to each pilot. One will be retained, and one will be signed and returned.

Pilots Signature . . . .   *Date* . . . .

"COME IN N° 9 YOUR TIMES' UP"

WAIT HERE

"OK" the short straw takes her up first.

9 The Aviator and his Group

The best size for an aeroplane owning group is one, but since it is not possible always to maintain this number, plans must sometimes be laid to organise for larger groups.

I don't believe that it is very practical to operate a group of more than eight people as several could arrive simultaneously to fly – thus generating aggravation.

People forming a group have to understand from the beginning exactly what it is that they are sharing and it is rathermore than just flying.

They are sharing:–
1. The purchase and running costs of the aircraft.
2. The chores, like washing the aircraft and brushing the hangar, these are unskilled tasks.
3. The maintenance work if on the P.F.A. or L.A M.S.
4. The administration and paperwork, for example keeping logs, paying bills, collecting members cash etc.
5. The flying.

They will have to cope with and be tolerant of varying levels of skills and competence and also varying levels of willingness to perform the tasks.

It is not difficult to imagine the feelings of a group member arriving on a good flying day with every intention of wearing it out only to discover that another member has taken the opportunity to swap the tyres around.

Group aeroplanes like club aeroplanes tend to be used mostly on short local trips as there seem always to be other members waiting and wishing to use the aircraft.

Having discussed some of the snags let me now explain my ideas for the successful and amicable operation of a group.

I believe that if it is possible a group should be formed to share the running costs of an aeroplane and not share the purchasing cost.

It is better if the machine is owned by one individual than a group. This clearly places upon that individual the responsibilities of maintenance and administration, which means that no differences arise over the unequal sharing of these responsibilities as they are not shared. To set against this extra responsibility the owner reaps the benefit of any appreciation in the value of the aircraft and he has some help in the paying of the bills.

Also, since the ownership is clearly defined, no arguments can arise when it comes time to dispose of the aircraft and acquire a different one or to change or update any of its equipment.

The non owning participants do not need to make a capital investment but they are able to participate in the cheaper flying that usually arises from group operations and whatever the levels of their skills they can help in the 'wash and brush up department'.

Group rules should be clear and concise and each group member should be issued with two copies – one to keep and one to sign and return. It is also a good idea to send a copy to the insurers so that they are in no doubt as to the manner in which the group conducts its' business.

It must be remembered that rules are only called upon after trouble has arisen, either from the misconduct of an individual or worse, from an accident.

At the formation stage when all members are good

friends and looking forward eagerly to the prospect it may seem that rules will be unnecessary but Moses would not have needed the Commandments if everyone had intended to keep them anyway.

The P.F.A. actively encourages group ownership and the P.F.A. Handbook gives a set of model rules which can be used as a basis for forming up a set to suit the needs and circumstances of a particular group. Our own rules are reproduced elsewhere in this book and have served us well thus far.

The running costs can be divided into two parts.

1. The overheads which will have to be paid whether flying takes place or not — for example insurance and hangarage.
2. Costs arising from flying — for example fuel, oil and spares.

Number one should be estimated for a year and divided amongst the group and paid into the aeroplane account monthly as a fixed charge to be paid whether the member flies or not.

Number two should be estimated on a per hour basis and paid into the account monthly according to the hours flown by each member. The member in the left seat is the one who is responsible for the payment.

If a member buys from his own pocket fuel or spare parts the receipts for these purchases should be handed in and be credited against that member's flying account.

Choosing the aircraft is every bit as important as choosing the members of the group. It must be chosen:—

1. To suit the environment in which it will be operated, for example farmers field or licensed airfield.
2. The purpose for which it will be required, for example, local hop, aerobatics, continental touring or training.

3.   The number of seats.
4.   Certificate of Airworthiness or Permit to fly.
5.   Metal structure or wood structure.
6.   Ability to carry or be adapted for Avionics.
7.   Single engine or twin.
8.   Covered or open cockpit.
9.   American or British engine.
10. Tricycle or taildragger.
11. High or low wing (This can make a considerable difference to the cost of hangar construction).

Examining these points a little closer let us consider first the operating environment.

All aircraft can be safely operated from a licensed airfield with hard runways and aprons, but this is not quite the case when you are flying from a farmer's field. Usually a taildragger e.g., a Jodel or a Piper Cub are best suited to a grass field with a rough surface. That nose leg is very vulnerable and if a taildragger doesn't taxi or steer so well on the ground a burst of power usually sets you pointing in the right direction and is safer applied on a grass field than on a hard taxi way.

The position of the wing is an environmental consideration as a high wing usually escapes being splattered with cow muck when you use a pasture field. A low wing will get the lot on both upper and lower surfaces, thus letting the pilot in for several hours of uncomfortable work. The number of seats is also an environmental consideration as the take off distance required by a fully loaded four place is a great deal more than for a fully loaded two place, and of course the resistance of wheels through grass is much greater than over concrete – so a four place is not really a practical proposition for farm strip flying.

Everyone wishes to fly for a different reason so with a group there may be a group of reasons if you are not very careful.

A Chipmunk would be a good choice for a group interested in aerobatics, but would be an expensive touring or training aeroplane.

A suitable touring aeroplane with a good short field performance would be any of the two place Jodels.

A Luton Minor with its open cockpit would not find many takers on a frosty morning and would not be a very practical plane for a continental tour.

If some members of the proposed group are skilled and reliable engineers a Permit aircraft on the P.F.A. is a very good proposition. This does not of course mean that maintenance is done cheaply because it may be neglected. Maintenance must not only be done, it must be seen to be done and the work must be of a high and painstaking standard for a considerable period before your inspector develops a trust and confidence in your ability to cope.

Usually a permit can be granted on a two place aircraft not exceeding 125 HP and weighing less than 1750 lbs. But you cannot train on permit aircraft.

All other aircraft must be maintained to Light Aircraft Maintenance Schedules by a licensed engineer and he must of course be paid.

Concessions can be obtained on aircraft operated in the private category e.g. engines are not limited to a set number of hours between overhauls, but may continue to run provided regular tests are made to ensure that they remain in good condition. An aircraft operated in the private category may be used for training but not for hire and reward.

I personally favour a wooden aeroplane, but that is

hardly surprising as I am a carpenter and joiner and therefore find inspections and repairs relatively easy. For another skilled in metal work the reverse may be true. If your proposed group is going to need professional help for repairs and maintenance you should scout your locality to discover the types of services available to you. You will be surprised how few repair shops will undertake repairs on wood and fabric aircraft.

The avionics scene has changed dramatically in recent years, both in the nature of the boxes and in the advantages obtained in their use.

While it is not vital to have communications, radios, VOR, ADF and a Transponder indeed many people fight hard to maintain their right to fly without them and I uphold them if that is their wish. My own view is that anything that helps me to avoid being lost or enables me safely to transit a piece of controlled airspace without the added risk of incurring a controllers anger I must have, and my experience is that many of my journeys have been shortened by direct crossing of C.T.R.'s which have only been possible with the aid of my Transponder and indeed it is no exaggeration to say that on one occasion it saved my life.

In recent years the boxes have been miniaturised and lightened to the extent that they can be fitted into most aeroplanes, even their reduced use of current has brought them within the scope of the generators fitted to the smaller American flat four engines. It is quite common nowadays to see a 360 channel radio running from rechargeable motorcycle batteries quite successfully. I have recently observed a small wind driven generator fitted to an aircraft that has no engine driven one.

On the question of engines, it is generally accepted

that the American flat four engines both Lycoming and Continental are cheaper to run and maintain than their British in-line counterparts, spares being more readily available and cheaper. This is a sad fact, but one we must live with. Also 100 LL fuel is not liked much by the low compression engines e.g., Continental A65 C90 and I believe that the British engines like it even less. Generally groups are formed around single engined aeroplanes for the obvious reason that groups are usually formed for the purpose of providing cheaper flying and twins are not cheap to fly.

As far as the accounts are concerned I favour a simple system which uses as its basis the AOPA Record of Flight sheets. This is pinned in the hangar and is used for booking out, recording fuel uplift quantities and by whom. Notice of defects and their correction, brief repairs and maintenance notes and of course journey destinations and flight times.

From this last a simple account is kept and balanced at each month end and that balance paid by that member with the account being credited with a payment being made by that member on behalf of the group.

The group fund is administered in a similar way with the payments from members to group being shown in credit column and payments out being on the debit side, whether from an individual member or with a cheque from the group account. Group cheques being required to be signed by at least two group members as a safeguard and I reproduce below a short section of an individual members flying account and the aeroplane maintenance account.

DATE	ITEM	CREDIT	DEBIT
1. 7. 80	Opening Balance	422.17	
2. 7. 80	Fencer Battery Mr A. Cash Purchase		13.36
3. 7. 80	Hangar Paint Mr B. "		12.95
9. 7. 80	Fuel - Sleap Mr A. "		23.10
15. 7. 80	Fuel - Barton Mr B. "		34.27
24. 7. 80	Fuel & Oil, Sywell Mr A. "		14.68
29. 7. 80	Paid into Bank Mr B. "	77.21	
	CLOSING BALANCE		401.02
		499.38	499.38
1. 8. 80	Opening Balance	401.02	
3. 8. 80	Paid into bank Mr A.	25.00	
5. 8. 80	Tail Spring Repair Mr A. Cash Purchase		13.14
6. 8. 80	Fuel - Sleap Mr B. "		27.69
9. 8. 80	Fuel - Blackpool Mr A. "		16.27
15. 8. 80	Radio Repair Group Cheque		34.19
19. 8. 80	Fuel - Sleap Mr A. Cash Purchase		25.17
30. 8. 80	Paid into Bank Mr B.	50.00	
	CLOSING BALANCE		359.56
		476.02	476.02

EXTRACT FROM AIRCRAFT ACCOUNT

DATE	ITEM	CREDIT	DEBIT
1. 7. 80	Opening Balance	38.67	
2. 7. 80	Fencer Battery Cash Purchase	13.36	
9. 7. 80	Fuel - Sleap "	23.10	
24. 7. 80	Fuel & oil - Sywell "	14.68	
31. 7. 80	Standing Charge - JULY		16.00
31. 7. 80	Flying Charge 8.58 hrs at £11.50		98.67
	CLOSING BALANCE	24.86	
		114.67	114.67
1. 8. 80	Opening Balance		24.86
3. 8. 80	Paid into Bank	25.00	
5. 8. 80	Tail Spring Repair Cash Purchase	13.14	
9. 8. 80	Fuel - Blackpool "	16.27	
19. 8. 80	Fuel - Sleap "	25.17	
31. 8. 80	Standing Charge - AUGUST		16.00
31. 8. 80	Flying Charge 6.71 hrs at £11.50		77.16
	CLOSING BALANCE	38.44	
		118.02	118.02
1. 9. 80	Opening Balance		38.44

TYPICAL GROUP MEMBER'S MONTHLY ACCOUNT

10 The Undesignated Airfield

Few restrictions are placed upon people aviating from undesignated airfields, unless they are within or beneath a C.T.R. There is one restriction however that should be understood.

You should know that it is illegal to fly from a private strip direct to any offshore island of the U.K. No, it is nothing to do with Customs. The recent Anti-Terrorist Act is the culprit. You must call at a 'designated' (with Police and Customs) airfield both outgoing and incoming, to obtain a security clearance. Do not expect to have your landing fees paid for you by the Police either! You detour entirely at your own expense.

There is however another way. The Act provides that the Chief Constable may give a security clearance for you to fly direct from your strip. You must write to him and give him details of your proposed flight, giving him sufficient notice, since he is likely to send a C.I.D. chappie to check upon your political affiliations. Having satisfied himself he will write and give his approval to the flight and if he is like my Chief Constable, he will not wish to supervise the flight.

Subsequent flights will simply be a matter of writing for an approval, the visit being dispensed with.

I strongly recommend that you do not make a direct flight without making these arrangements or, like me, you may be met at your destination by two determined looking burly gentlemen dressed in black who took a lot of convincing that I had no *Gelly* aboard.

A letter form the Chief Constable has served me well, during several visits to the Isle of Mann T.T. Races.

I recommend the procedure and reproduce my written request and the reply.

The Lilacs,
Kinsey Heath,
Audlem,
Crewe,
Cheshire.
27th April, 1976.

The Chief Administrative Officer,
Cheshire Constabulary,
Crewe,
Cheshire.

Dear Sir,

In regard to the prevention of terrorism (supplemental temporary provisions) order 1976 (SI 1976 No. 465 and the prevention of terrorism (supplemental temporary provisions) (Northern Ireland) order 1976 (SI 1976 No. 466)

I wish to apply to you under the provisions and conditions of the above Order for supervision of a flight I intend to make in my private aircraft from a non designated airfield at Austerson Dairy Farm, Nantwich on Friday, 11th June 1976. The purpose of the flight is to attend the T.T. Races at the Isle of Man and I intend to leave Austerson Dairy Farm and fly direct to Ronaldsway.

Weather permitting the flight will commence at 8.30 a.m. and the supervision will also be required for the return flight which should end at Austerson Dairy Farm at approximately 7.00 p.m. on that same day.

I thank you in anticipation.

Yours faithfully,
G. H. Farr.

Cheshire Constabulary

Mr. G H Farr
The Lilacs
Kinsey Heath
Audlem
CREWE   Cheshire

Chief Constable's Office
Constabulary Headquarters
Chester CHI 2PP
Telephone Chester 51222
Telex 61941

If you telephone please ask for

Mr Woodcock

Our reference	Tel. extension	Your reference	Date
CW/GP	201		14 May 1976

Dear Sir

I refer to your letter dated 27 April 1976 addressed to the Chief
Superintendent at Crewe, which has been passed to this office for
attention.

The Chief Constable has no objection to your intention to fly your
private aircraft from a non-designated airfield at Austerson Dairy Farm,
Nantwich, on Friday 11 June 1976, and to return later that evening.
It is understood that the only passenger to be travelling on the aircraft
will be your wife.   It is not intended that your departure or return
will be supervised by the police and you may accept this letter as
authority for the purposes of the legislation relating to the prevention
of terrorism.

Yours faithfully

Assistant Chief Constable - Operations

All correspondence invoking our reference shown above to be addressed to the Chief Constable

Finally I should tell you that to become a country aviator, you must not be of faint heart for you must be entirely self-sufficient.

You have no engineer to call over to your aeroplane. You have no fire or rescue services. You are entirely responsible for deciding when it is fit or not fit to fly.

Many of the services, support, control and guidance available to the town flier are not available to you. You will dip your own oil and kick your own tyres. But the freedom from all sorts of Big Brothers is something to be savoured and I know of few things that give me more pleasure.

Much of what you have read may seem unorthodox, but to survive as a country flyer you have to be a little unorthodox.

You will make some mistakes, but not as many as I have done. I sincerely hope you will have fun.

In the sh..t again

75

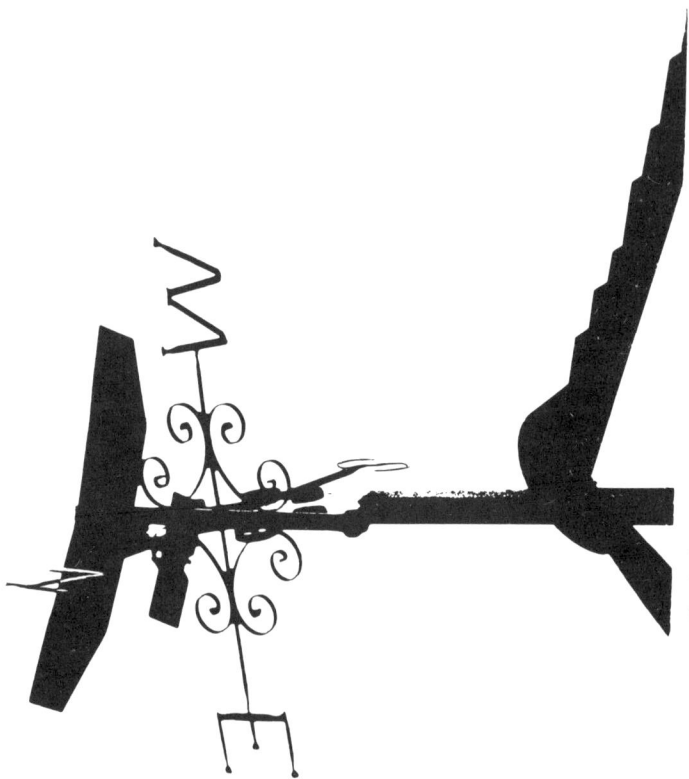

Check the wind direction BEFORE leaving home